Original title:

Jasmine Mires Under the Unicorn Turf

Copyright © 2025 Swan Charm

Author: Eliora Lumiste

ISBN HARDBACK: 978-1-80562-784-5

ISBN PAPERBACK: 978-1-80564-305-0

Revelations Within the Meadow's Embrace

In the meadow green and bright,
Whispers dance with morning light.
Secrets linger in the air,
Nature's song, a tender prayer.

Petals glisten with soft dew,
Every color, a dream anew.
Butterflies twirl, spirits free,
A glimpse of what's meant to be.

Hidden paths where shadows play,
Echoes of a bygone day.
Ancient trees with stories deep,
Guardians of the roots they keep.

Softly, time begins to bend,
Winding roads that never end.
In each heartbeat, truth reveals,
Life unfolds, and magic heals.

With every breeze that sweeps the field,
Hearts untouched, their fate concealed.
Glimmers of joy that softly swell,
In secrets kept, we learn to tell.

As the Unicorns Fly Amongst the Stars

A sky ablaze with glimmering lights,
Whispers echo through the nights.
Unicorns dance on silver beams,
Chasing after ancient dreams.

With manes that shimmer, tails like silk,
They ride the starlit ocean's milk.
Clutched by magic's gentle hand,
In ethereal realms, they stand.

Across the cosmos, they will stride,
A celestial parade, in joy, they glide.
Each hoof a comet, each sigh a star,
Together, they soar, forever far.

In the heart of this radiant high,
Hope ignites, as dreamers cry.
For in the realms of wonder vast,
The future glimmers, bright and fast.

So let your spirit take to flight,
Amongst the stars, in endless night.
For when you believe, you shall perceive,
The magic that our dreams can weave.

Shadows of the Mythic Deer

In twilight's hush, the whispers creep,
Where moonlight dances, secrets keep.
With antlers crowned by silver rays,
The deer of myth in misty glaze.

They roam through glades where dreams align,
In shimmering coats, their forms divine.
With every step, the wild hearts race,
In shadows cast, they find their place.

Among the trees, the stories weave,
Of lives entwined, we dare believe.
In silent woods, they lead the way,
To realms where night embraces day.

Their calls resound, a haunting sound,
In echoes born from ancient ground.
The mythic deer, forever near,
In twilight's glow, we hold them dear.

Treading Softly on Fantastical Lawn

Upon the grass where fairies tread,
In secret realms where dreams are fed.
A tapestry of colors bright,
Awakens softly in the night.

With every step, the whispers rise,
Of playful sprites beneath the skies.
Each blade of dew, a world to see,
While moonlit shadows dance with glee.

The flowers hum a gentle tune,
Beneath the watchful gaze of moon.
In softest glades where wonders play,
Our hearts are light, we drift away.

Among the blooms both rare and fine,
We trace the paths where stardust shines.
In every breath, magic's embrace,
We find our joy in nature's grace.

Echoes of Celestial Blooms

Beneath the stars, the flowers gleam,
In fragrant breaths, we chase a dream.
Their colors swirl like painted skies,
Awakening hope in weary eyes.

Each petal holds a secret thread,
Of tales long lost, of dreams once fed.
In gardens rich with whispered lore,
We wander forth to seek and explore.

The heavens speak through blossoms bright,
In twilight's hush, in soft moonlight.
They share the tales of distant lands,
In each bouquet, a magic stands.

With every bloom, a wish reborn,
In echoes soft, the night adorns.
Celestial blooms, a guiding light,
In hearts of those who dare take flight.

Guardians of Ethereal Fields

In fields where stars weave golden threads,
The guardians watch as daylight spreads.
With eyes like pools of ancient skies,
They guard the dreams that never die.

Through twilight's veil, their spirits roam,
In every whisper, they call us home.
With gentle hands, they guide our way,
Through shadowed glades where fairies play.

In ethereal light, they softly shine,
In realms where fate and dreams entwine.
With every step, the magic flows,
In fields where time forever glows.

Guardians bold, with hearts so wide,
In every soul, they bide their tide.
In unity, we hear their song,
In ethereal fields, we all belong.

Whispers from the Ethereal Glade

In the depths where shadows dance,
Whispers float like dreams entranced.
Leaves that shimmer, soft and bright,
Guard the secrets of the night.

Moonlight weaves a silver thread,
Binding tales of those who tread.
Ancient trees with stories old,
Nestle wisdom, soft and bold.

Echoes of forgotten lore,
Through the glade's enchanting door.
Crickets sing their nightly song,
Calling all to join along.

Time stands still beneath the stars,
Woven dreams in silver jars.
Nature hums a lullaby,
As the fireflies flicker by.

In each rustle, in each sigh,
Magic dwells, it cannot lie.
Hear the whispers, close your eyes,
Let your spirit learn to rise.

The Magic of Lush Dreams

In fields where vibrant flowers bloom,
Lies a world that weaves with gloom.
Innocent sighs and laughter play,
Chasing shadows of the day.

Whirling winds bring tales of old,
In sweet aromas, bright and bold.
Every petal holds a spark,
Filling hearts against the dark.

Nestled deep in the heart of green,
A tapestry of sights unseen.
Drifting thoughts on breezes glide,
Where the wild fairy folk reside.

Glistening dew on morning's breath,
Carries whispers of life and death.
In this realm of vibrant dreams,
Nothing's ever as it seems.

Beneath the arch of willow's sway,
Time slips gently, finds its play.
Every moment, pure and rare,
Casts a spell upon the air.

Journey Through the Mystic Vale

Across the hills, the shadows creep,
In the vale where secrets sleep.
Paths entwined in shimmering mist,
Holding tales not to be missed.

The brook shall guide with babbling cheer,
Drawing wanderers ever near.
Twilight waltzes with the light,
Crafting wonders through the night.

Every turn brings wonder bright,
With echoes of a distant fight.
Ancient stones in quiet repose,
Veil the tales nobody knows.

Breath of magic fills the air,
Each bold heart learns to dare.
Through these lands of whispered dreams,
Time unravels at its seams.

In the twilight's soft embrace,
Every step finds its own place.
As the stars begin to sing,
Hope is born on silver wing.

Starlit Reveries on the Green

Where the grass meets evening's glow,
Starlit dreams in soft wind flow.
Beneath the sky, a canvas wide,
In the hush, our hearts abide.

Crickets play their joyous tune,
Underneath the watchful moon.
Every whisper carries light,
Guiding souls through velvet night.

Woven tales of land and sea,
Guide the way for you and me.
With each glance at twinkling skies,
Magic night uncovers lies.

Laughter echoes, pure and clear,
Kindling warmth for those who cheer.
Upon the green, we drift and sway,
In our hearts, the magic stays.

Dreamers gather, hand in hand,
In a world that's softly planned.
With each star, a wish is born,
In the light of early morn.

Dreams Drift on Starry Dew

In twilight's hush, the stars awake,
Soft whispers float on night's cool breath.
The moonlight weaves a silken path,
Where dreams embrace the world beneath.

Each twinkling spark, a wish set free,
A gentle waltz on velvet skies.
Through silver beams, our hopes will soar,
As shadows dance, our spirits rise.

In secret glades, where magic hides,
The melodies of fate align.
With every beat, our hearts will sing,
As stardust weaves through space and time.

Awake, beloved, the night is young,
With every breath, new tales are spun.
Let laughter echo, pure and bright,
For dreams drift soft, like dew on dawn.

So close your eyes, and take my hand,
Together, we'll explore the night.
A tapestry of wonder waits,
As dreams drift softly into flight.

Comfort of the Forgotten Fields

Where wildflowers bloom and whispers dwell,
In fields untouched by time's embrace.
The breeze carries tales of old,
Of laughter lost, and love's warm grace.

Beneath the oak, a secret lies,
In shadows cast by nature's might.
The sun dips low with gentle sighs,
In twilight's glow, our hearts take flight.

Rustling reeds, a lullaby,
The crickets join in evening's song.
Each memory breathed, like earth and sky,
In forgotten fields where we belong.

A symphony of rustling leaves,
Their whispers weave a tapestry.
In this embrace, our sorrows ease,
The fields hold deep serenity.

So let us wander hand in hand,
Through golden grass and skies of blue.
In nature's heart, we'll seek to find,
The comfort that was born anew.

The Gleam of Wishes Unspoken

In the quiet hour when twilight winks,
Amidst the sigh of dreamers' breaths,
A flicker glows, a thought unchained,
The gleam of wishes, softly blessed.

With every heartbeat, desires bloom,
Like petals sprouting from the dark.
Each silent hope, a whispered tune,
That dances in the night's sweet spark.

The yearning souls beneath the stars,
Unravel tales of longing deep.
Each gleam ignites, like distant Mars,
In hearts that hold the dreams we keep.

So speak the words your heart won't say,
Let constellations guide the way.
For every wish, when cast in light,
Will twinkle through the endless night.

In starlit realms, where echoes fade,
The magic swirls, a radiant veil.
Wishes soar, though none are made,
In silence, they weave their ethereal trail.

A Dance in Faery's Embrace

Beneath the boughs of ancient groves,
Where shadows play and secrets gleam,
The faeries twirl on petals soft,
In a dance that whispers like a dream.

With giggles bright like morning dew,
They weave their magic through the night.
In spirals of starlight, they beckon us,
To join their revels, pure delight.

The moonlight bathes the enchanted ground,
While music drifts on evening's air.
In elfin flesh, the world unwound,
A fleeting glimpse of magic rare.

So let us sway, our spirits bare,
As laughter rings through emerald trees.
In every step, a wish laid bare,
A fleeting freedom, nature's keys.

When dawn's light breaks, we bid farewell,
Yet in our hearts, the memory stays.
For once we danced with faeries fair,
In twilight's glow, our souls ablaze.

A Voyage Through Whispering Flora

In a glimmering glade where shadows play,
Petals flutter softly, in hues of jade.
A song of the breeze, whispers secrets anew,
Calling forth dreams in morning's dew.

Through thickets of thyme, a path unfolds,
With stories of old wrapped in marigold.
Each rustle, a riddle; each leaf, a guide,
In the heart of the forest, where wonders abide.

Gossamer trails of shimmering light,
Dancing through branches, a delicate flight.
With every turn taken, a new sight to behold,
Adventures await, like treasures untold.

Underneath the starlit tapestry bright,
Creatures emerge in the velvet night.
The blooms start to chatter, sharing their lore,
As the voyage unfolds, revealing much more.

So follow the whispers, let curiosity steer,
In gardens enchanted, where magic is near.
Through fragrant enchantments, let your heart soar,
For each step in the glade opens a new door.

Celestial Gardens of the Unseen

Beyond the horizon, where dreams take flight,
Lie gardens of starlight, in shimmering night.
Each blossom a beacon, a story they tell,
Of worlds intertwined within silence's spell.

The moon weaves a tapestry, silver and grand,
As the petals unfurl, like wishes unplanned.
In hidden corners, where shadows may creep,
Secrets of cosmos lie quiet, and deep.

With each gentle breeze, the universe sings,
A melody crafted on soft feathered wings.
Whispers in twilight, soft echoes of grace,
Invite you to wander through time and through space.

Oceans of beauty, where stardust can play,
In the heart of the garden, the night turns to day.
With wonders and marvels that shimmer and gleam,
Awake in the moment, the world feels a dream.

Let your heart flourish in this timeless domain,
For the celestial gardens will soothe every pain.
Unseen yet so vibrant, they flourish and swoon,
In realms of enchantment beneath the pale moon.

The Tapestry of Hidden Wonders

In the folds of the earth, where mysteries weave,
Lie wonders that whisper, if you just believe.
Threads of enchantment, both humble and grand,
Woven in silence by nature's own hand.

Through valleys and mountains, where secrets are hid,
Ancient tales linger, in shadows they slid.
Each flower a color, each stone bears a name,
In the tapestry woven, all life plays the game.

The gentle brook's laughter, a soft, soothing sound,
Guiding the wanderers lost, yet spellbound.
With each step we take, new wonders ignite,
The fabric of life revealed in the light.

Beneath the vast sky, in the hush of the night,
The tapestry unfurls, a marvelous sight.
In every small detail, there lies a surprise,
In the quiet and stillness, our spirits arise.

So gather your courage and venture ahead,
For the hidden wonders await, just as said.
In the tapestry's warmth, let your spirit be free,
A dance with the magic, just you and the sea.

Petals and Hooves of Curiosity

When daylight breaks through, in vibrant array,
Hooves tread on soft grass, where wildflowers sway.
Petals unfold gently, a colorful spree,
Inviting the wanderers, come dance with me.

Curious creatures, both feathered and furred,
Share whispers of wonders, their tales undeterred.
Every corner explored, a story to tell,
In the meadow's embrace, where mysteries dwell.

With the rustle of leaves, excitement is born,
As hooves tap a rhythm, greeting the dawn.
Adventures await where the sky meets the land,
In the petals of flora, and the warmth of the sand.

So roam through the garden, let curiosity reign,
With each joyous leap, feel the wildness unchain.
A symphony blooms in the heart of the land,
Where petals and hooves create magic, so grand.

In this dance of delight, let your spirit unwind,
For in nature's embrace, true treasures you'll find.
With petals and hooves, take a breath, feel the thrill,
In the realm of curiosity, let your heart fill.

Whispers in the Enchanted Meadow

In the meadow where magic sighs,
Where daisies dance under open skies,
The whispers of fairies flit and weave,
Crafting secrets that none can perceive.

Beneath the boughs of a grand, old oak,
Lost in the tales that the wind once spoke,
The brook babbles softly, a gentle tune,
A lullaby kissed by the silver moon.

Fields of lavender, sweet and bright,
Glow softly under the starlit night,
While shadows play on the soft green grass,
In the enchanted moments that swiftly pass.

Time slips away in this perfect dream,
Where kindness lingers in every beam,
Where each petal holds a glimpse of fate,
In the meadow where heartbeats contemplate.

So wander here, let your spirit soar,
Through whispers of magic, forevermore,
For in this haven, where dreams are spun,
The enchanted meadow calls everyone.

The Veil of Unicorn Dreams

A veil of mist on a starlit night,
Hides the realm of pure delight,
Where unicorns graze in silver streams,
Guarding the path to forgotten dreams.

With hooves that tread on ethereal ground,
They dance to the music, soft and profound,
Their manes aglow with the softest light,
Echoing whispers of the ancient night.

In this domain where heartbeats blend,
Magic and wonder have no end,
Each twinkle above tells a tale anew,
Of journeys taken and wishes true.

So close your eyes, let the wonders rise,
Beyond the horizon, where spirit flies,
In the embrace of enchantment's scheme,
You'll find the glow of unicorn dreams.

With every sunrise that paints the dawn,
The magic whispers, though dreams are gone,
Yet in your heart, let the magic stay,
For unicorns linger in light's soft clay.

Beneath Velvet Petals

Beneath the petals of velvet hue,
Secrets of nature come into view,
As twilight descends with a gentle grace,
Each blossom unveils a hidden place.

The fragrance twirls like a silken thread,
Where dreams are woven, and whispers spread,
Though mysterious shadows drift through the air,
Each moment whispers, enchantments to share.

In twilight's glow, the softest sighs,
Spin tales of magic that never dies,
The stars peek through the lace of night,
Guiding lost souls in their quiet flight.

So linger below this canopy bright,
Let go of worries and take to flight,
For beneath velvet petals, dreams unfold,
A world of wonders and stories untold.

In every color that the flowers hold,
There lies a promise, a tale of old,
Beneath these petals, your heart will find,
The magic whispered by nature's kind.

Sylvan Secrets in Moonlight

In the heart of the woods where shadows play,
Secrets unfold in a mystical way,
Beneath the gaze of the silver moon,
The forest sings its enchanting tune.

Whispers of creatures, both great and small,
Echo through trees that stand proud and tall,
Every breeze carries a timeless lore,
Of fairies circling on a twilight floor.

The canopy sparkles with glimmers bright,
As dew-kissed leaves catch the softest light,
A haven where mysteries softly breathe,
In sylvan secrets that the night weaves.

So lose your way on this moonlit trail,
Where every shadow tells a hidden tale,
And let the magic of night be your guide,
Through sylvan secrets where wonders abide.

For each rustle and sigh in this sacred glen,
Holds the whispers of nature, time and again,
In such moments, your spirit finds grace,
In sylvan secrets, you've found your place.

Moonlight and Mythic Magic

Beneath the shimmering moon's bright glow,
Whispers of magic in the night do flow.
Mysteries dance in shadows so deep,
Awakening dreams that wander and leap.

Wands of willow weave tales untold,
Secrets of starlight in stories unfold.
A world where enchantment reigns supreme,
Spinning the fabric of each fleeting dream.

In gardens where faeries flit and play,
Beneath ancient oaks at the close of day.
Laughter and whispers swirl on the breeze,
Inviting all hearts to find sweet release.

Olive branches cradle the soft night air,
Lunar kisses weaving through silken hair.
Magic ignites with each glimmering spark,
Illuminating paths in the soft, endless dark.

With every heartbeat, the cosmos aligns,
In moonlight's embrace, all longing entwines.
Mythic and wild, the magic awakes,
A journey of wonder that the heart makes.

The Dust of Long-Lost Legends

In the attic where shadows layer the floor,
Dusty tomes whisper of times long before.
Pages that crackle like dried autumn leaves,
Each word a doorway, where fancy believes.

Knights in shining armor, fierce and bold,
Speaking of quests that are yet to unfold.
Ghosts of the past linger close and near,
Their tales a chorus we long to hear.

Echoes of laughter ringing through halls,
Faded portraits down ancient stone walls.
The power of stories that reach through the years,
If listened to closely, can banish our fears.

Metallic gleams of a dragon's lost hoard,
Cloaked in the shadows of tales unexplored.
Time's gentle fingers brush over each line,
As secrets awaken, an age-old design.

From scrolls and fragments, the legends arise,
Resurrected through dreams and twilight skies.
The dust of the past swirls in the light,
Reviving the magic that once took flight.

Tales from the Verdant Veil

Deep in the forest, where echoes reside,
Emerald whispers the wind cannot hide.
Secrets of nature, entwined in the trees,
Carried on currents, like soft autumn breeze.

Branches cradle stories of creatures bright,
Elusive and shy, in the soft golden light.
Magic of moss and the shimmer of dew,
A tapestry woven in every hue.

Rivers that giggle over smooth, polished stone,
Guarding the tales of the wild unknown.
Creatures of magic with hearts bold and free,
Gathering 'round roots of the elder tree.

Songs of the nightingale rise with the dawn,
Echoing softly as shadows are drawn.
The verdant veil whispers its ancient tune,
As stars gently bow to the sun and the moon.

Beneath leafy canopies, dreams take their flight,
In the heart of the woods, where all feels just right.
Tales from the verdant, where legends are spun,
In the melody shared by the earth and the sun.

Enigma in the Emerald Enclosure

In the heart of the glade, where the shadows meld,
A mystery dwells, in the silence compelled.
Emerald curtains drape skies that confound,
Whispers of magic enclose all around.

Hidden in flowers, the enchantments do bloom,
Silent secrets drift through the emerald gloom.
Crickets are strumming a lullaby sweet,
Dancing in moonlight, the fairies retreat.

Pathways that weave like thoughts in a dream,
Beneath tangled branches, the sunlight can gleam.
Footsteps of wanderers, long left behind,
In this sacred space, all the lost souls unwind.

Fog rolls like whispers, gentle and light,
Wrapping the trees in a cloak of the night.
The enigma deepens with each echoing breath,
Alive in the stillness, a dance with the death.

Cloaked in the shadows, the wonders unfurl,
Revealing the magic that makes the heart whirl.
In this emerald enclosure, all life feels anew,
Cruising through secrets the forest imbues.

The Allure of Untold Stories

Whispers weave through shadows deep,
Secrets slumber, dreams to keep.
Tales of magic, joy, and woe,
In every heart, they long to grow.

Through ancient tomes and twilight glow,
Pages turn, the wonders flow.
Heroes rise, and fables fade,
In their realms, new lives are made.

Beneath the stars, a spark ignites,
Adventures born on moonlit nights.
Voices call from bygone lands,
In every tale, a thread of hands.

So gather 'round, let stories start,
A journey filled with boundless heart.
For every end begins anew,
In every word, a glimpse of you.

The allure of what's never told,
Awaits in shadows, bright and bold.
With every chapter, whispers play,
Inviting souls to dance and sway.

Echoes of Nature's Grace

In rustling leaves, the breezes sing,
The dance of life, a gentle fling.
Mountains echo, valleys sigh,
Nature's grace will never die.

The sun paints skies in hues divine,
In every flower, stories twine.
Rivers whisper, rocks stand tall,
In harmony, they heed the call.

Morning's dew on blades of green,
A sparkling tapestry, unseen.
Birds take flight, the world awakes,
Nature's art, a love that stakes.

With every heartbeat, nature breathes,
In every bud, new life weaves.
Her whispers echo through the vale,
In every journey, we unveil.

So let the wild teach us its song,
In every note, we all belong.
For in the grace of all we see,
Nature's echo sets us free.

Flight of the Imagination's Wings

Across the skies, the dreams take flight,
With every thought, igniting light.
Imagination paints the air,
Creating worlds beyond compare.

The mind can soar where eagles dare,
In visions bright, we find our share.
Through realms unseen, we venture far,
Guided by our inner star.

Castles built on clouds of cream,
Adventure flows, a vibrant stream.
Valid and wild, the heartbeats race,
In every corner, finding grace.

With every flutter, dreams take form,
In whispered tales, in visions warm.
A tapestry of hopes unfurled,
Unlimits the horizons of our world.

So let your spirit learn to fly,
On wings of wonder, touch the sky.
For in the flight of thought's embrace,
We find our meaning, our true place.

The Secret in the Verdant Tides

In emerald waves where secrets sway,
The lull of nature calls to play.
Beneath the boughs, a mystery lies,
A world unseen beneath the skies.

Wildflowers dance in gentle streams,
Carrying whispers of hidden dreams.
Life pulses on in silver streams,
And every ripple holds our schemes.

The heartbeat of the earth runs deep,
In verdant tides, our spirits leap.
Where shadows play and sunlight gleams,
The secret thrives in nature's beams.

So venture forth, let courage rise,
To seek the truth beyond the lies.
In every whisper, feel the grace,
The secret blooms in nature's embrace.

And as the sun begins to set,
Remember all that we forget.
In dense green woods and twists of vine,
The secrets bind, your heart and mine.

Elysian Echoes of Nature's Heart

In emerald glades where whispers weave,
The trees hold secrets, soft and sweet.
With every breeze, a tale takes flight,
In nature's heart, the world feels right.

The brook sings songs of ages past,
While sunbeams dance on dewdrops cast.
Each leaf a note in symphony,
Resounding life in harmony.

With petals bright in colors rare,
The flowers bloom with fragrant flair.
A tapestry of sights and sounds,
In Elysium, pure joy abounds.

The hills invite with arms so wide,
Where dreams and hopes like rivers glide.
Each step reveals a wondrous scene,
Nature's magic, sweet and green.

Journeys Through the Twilight Field

As shadows stretch and daylight fades,
The twilight field in silence wades.
With lantern lights that start to glow,
Each path reveals what we don't know.

The stars peek out with playful glee,
While night unfolds its mystery.
In gentle breeze, the whispers call,
To venture far, to fear and fall.

The moonlit road awaits our tread,
Filled with the dreams that we once fed.
In every corner, stories creep,
Through twilight's arms, we leap and sweep.

Seek visions where the shadows play,
In this enchanted, dusky sway.
Each moment held, a fleeting chance,
In twilight's grasp, we find our dance.

The Music of Falling Petals

When springtime's breath draws near to bloom,
The petals fall, a sweet perfume.
They dance upon the wind's soft sigh,
In harmony, they twirl and fly.

Each blossom tells a story bright,
Of love and loss, of day and night.
As pastel colors quilt the ground,
The earth holds secrets, beauty found.

Soft melodies in rustling trees,
Invite the heart to hear the breeze.
With every petal that descends,
A moment's magic never ends.

The music plays, a gentle tune,
That echoes softly 'neath the moon.
In gardens where the petals fall,
The world transforms, it beckons all.

Farewell to the Daydreaming Sky

The sun dips low, a golden sigh,
Farewell to the daydreaming sky.
With hues of blush and violet grace,
It paints the clouds, a soft embrace.

As twilight whispers its sweet refrain,
The stars emerge, a silver chain.
With every twinkle, tales unfold,
Of wishes cast and dreams retold.

The horizon blushes with soft delight,
As darkness wraps the world in night.
In silence, joy and peace conspire,
To kindle hearts with gentle fire.

So let us soar on wings of thought,
And capture all the dreams we sought.
Farewell for now, bright sunlit day,
In dreams we'll meet, come what may.

Luminous Footprints on Ethereal Soil

In twilight's embrace, the shadows play,
Soft glimmers of light pave the way.
Each step whispers secrets, age-old and wise,
As dreams take flight beneath twilight skies.

A forest of magic where echoes reside,
Through shimmering pathways, the spirits glide.
With every soft sigh, the night comes alive,
In a dance of wonder, the world will thrive.

The stars weave a tapestry, bright and bold,
Guiding lost travelers with stories untold.
Embraced by the night, we wander and roam,
Finding our way to a welcome home.

Luminous footprints, a trail of delight,
Leading us gently through whispers of night.
In each fleeting moment, a treasure we find,
In the stillness of time, our hearts intertwined.

So let us believe in this magical place,
Where shadows and starlight together embrace.
With every heartbeat, the rhythm we share,
Luminous footprints, our souls laid bare.

Starlight Danced 'Neath Ancient Boughs

Beneath the ancient boughs, where secrets sleep,
The starlight danced softly, the shadows deep.
Each flicker a promise of tales once spun,
In the heart of the woods, where time was undone.

Whispers of magic hung thick in the air,
With echoes of laughter that floated with care.
The moon painted silver on leaves like a dream,
In the hush of the night, we lost track of time's seam.

Amidst the entwined roots, the stories bloom,
Of faeries and fables that chase away gloom.
In the stillness, we listen, a symphony flows,
Through the heart of the forest, where wonder still grows.

Each star a reminder of wishes once made,
Illuminating pathways where hopes are laid.
As fireflies waltz in the velvety dark,
The woods cradle magic, igniting the spark.

So linger a moment, beneath the night's veil,
And let the starlight guide you through the pale.
For beneath ancient boughs, our hearts will embrace,
The beauty of night in this mystical place.

Whispers of the Eternal Glade

In the heart of the forest, a glade unfolds,
Where whispers of time dance, like stories retold.
Each rustling leaf sings of ages gone by,
Beneath the vast canvas of an ink-filled sky.

With petals like stardust, the flowers ignite,
The colors of magic, brilliant and bright.
In soft sighs of wind, the secrets emerge,
As nature's sweet hymn begins to converge.

The echoes of laughter weave through the trees,
Carried on currents that float with the breeze.
In the stillness, a promise is softly declared,
That dreams in the glade shall forever be shared.

Light filters softly through branches and leaves,
Kissing the earth where the old magic weaves.
In every shadow, a story shall thrive,
As the whispers of life feel eternally alive.

So linger here, traveler, take in the scene,
The splendor of nature, serene and pristine.
For within this glade, where time gently sways,
The whispers of forever shall always amaze.

A Serenade in the Sylvan Shade

When daylight retreats and dusk softly falls,
A serenade rises from nature's own halls.
The rustle of branches, a symphonic sigh,
As crickets resound beneath twilight's shy.

In the sylvan shade, where the wildflowers stand,
The melodies linger, creating a band.
With each gentle breeze, notes flutter and weave,
Weave stories of magic that hearts can believe.

Moonbeams descend like a silken embrace,
Glimmering softly on this enchanted place.
With starlight above and the earth 'neath our feet,
We dance to the rhythm, a joyous heartbeat.

In the hush of the night, the wonders unfold,
Revealing the secrets that nature has told.
With whispers of fables that glide on the air,
We're woven together, in dreams that we share.

So listen intently, dear wanderer bold,
In the sylvan shade where the stories are told.
For every sweet whisper and fluttering sound,
Is a serenade cherished where lost souls are found.

The Unwritten Lore of the Untamed

In shadows deep where whispers dwell,
Ancient tales begin to swell.
The wild beckons with luring grace,
Untraveled paths in an untouched place.

A dance of leaves, the breeze's sigh,
Where wild beasts roam and eagles fly.
Each rustle speaks of secrets held,
In nature's heart, where magic melds.

The moonlight weaves through branches high,
Illuminates the night sky's cry.
A tapestry of wonders spun,
In the realm where fables run.

Forgotten lore in every stone,
Stories ripe, yet all alone.
Time forgets, yet memories cling,
In a world where the wild things sing.

So tread with care on hallowed ground,
In untamed realms where dreams abound.
For every step a chance to find,
The unwritten lore of the untamed kind.

Harmonics in the Woodland Abode

In the heart of woods, a songbirds' trill,
Echoes through the glades, soft and shrill.
The trees sway with a rhythmic tune,
Beneath the watchful, silver moon.

Mossed stones whisper of days gone by,
Where echoes linger and spirits sigh.
Each note a balm for weary souls,
In harmony where magic rolls.

Sunlight dapples through the leaves,
Painting shadows, as nature weaves.
The brook hums low, a liquid sound,
In woodland halls, where peace is found.

Dreamers gather in twilight's embrace,
Sharing stories of time and space.
The woodland's voice, a gentle guide,
In this abode, where wonders hide.

Together we sing, hearts in tune,
With the tree's rustle and the crickets' croon.
In this sacred space, we're never alone,
For the woodland's song has found its home.

The Magic of Fragrant Memories

A whiff of jasmine, sweet and rare,
Awakens dreams from slumbered air.
Each petal's scent tells tales of yore,
Of laughter shared and love once more.

In gardens where the wildflowers bloom,
Life's fragrance spills, dispelling gloom.
The roses blush with stories old,
Of secrets shared and hearts of gold.

Breezes carry whispers soft,
Of cherished moments, rare and oft.
A waft of mint, a reminder bright,
Of childhood laughter under starlight.

Through the seasons, scents entwine,
In memory's dance, their magic shines.
Cinnamon warms the hearth of heart,
In fragrant swirls, we never part.

So take a breath, let memories flow,
In the magic of scents, we'll truly know.
For time may fade, but fragrances stay,
A tapestry of life, come what may.

Garden of the Heart's Whimsy

In a garden where wildflowers dream,
Whimsy dances in sunlight's gleam.
Petals brush against the sky,
With whispered secrets that flutter by.

Butterflies flit on silken wings,
In this haven where laughter springs.
Each bloom a note in playful rhyme,
A symphony of scents through time.

The lattice grows with ivy's twine,
Embracing tales of love divine.
Each corner holds a story told,
In this garden where dreams unfold.

Glistening dew beneath dawn's kiss,
In every drop, a taste of bliss.
Here, hearts bloom in colors bright,
Under the hush of soft starlight.

So wander through this treasured space,
Where whimsy wears a tender face.
In the garden of the heart's pure wish,
Magic blossoms in every swish.

Hopes Entwined with Wildflowers

In fields where sunlight spills and sways,
Wildflowers dance in soft arrays,
Each petal speaks of dreams untold,
In colors bright, they break the mold.

The whispers of the breeze, so sweet,
Caress the earth beneath my feet,
With every step, new hopes arise,
Like seeds that sprout beneath the skies.

The sky above, a canvas wide,
Where visions bloom, and fears subside,
A tapestry of dreams anew,
In nature's arms, my heart breaks through.

As twilight falls, the stars ignite,
The wildflowers shimmer in the night,
Their fragrant bloom, a beacon bright,
A promise held in quiet light.

So here I stand, where hopes align,
Among the blooms, our hearts entwine,
With every breath, a wish takes flight,
In endless dreams, we feel the light.

The Chronicles of Enchanted Realms

In lands where magic twines and glows,
Where ancient tales of wonder flow,
A tapestry of time unfolds,
In whispered lore, each heart beholds.

Beneath the trees with branches wide,
A unicorn swims in streams of pride,
And fairies flit on gossamer wings,
In every song the forest sings.

The moonlight casts a silver hue,
Upon the paths where dreams break through,
Each step reveals a story spun,
In twilight's grasp, our hearts are one.

A castle hidden in the mist,
Awaits the brave, the dreamers kissed,
With every stone, a tale of yore,
In enchanted realms, forevermore.

In shadows deep, the secrets lie,
With daring souls who never shy,
Their journeys weave through time and space,
In chronicles of love's embrace.

Echoes in Ethereal Air

In twilight's hush, a whisper calls,
An echo dances 'neath the walls,
Of crumbling towers lost to time,
Where shadows blend in whispered rhyme.

The wind carries tales of old,
In every note, a heart is bold,
As secrets glide on evening's breath,
In echoes that defy their death.

The stars emerge, a twinkling choir,
Each flicker fuels a deep desire,
For voices rise from dreams and fears,
In melodies of joy and tears.

A symphony of fates we meet,
In every heartbeat, every beat,
The world awakens, dancing free,
In echoes woven endlessly.

So here within the twilight's grace,
We find our rhythm, find our place,
As echoes linger in the air,
Reminding us that we still care.

Merriment Amidst the Verdant Whisper

In glades where laughter fills the day,
Amidst the leaves where children play,
A world alive, where dreams take flight,
In verdant whispers, pure delight.

The sunbeams kiss the emerald grass,
As breezes carry joys that pass,
With every giggle, life's renewed,
In nature's arms, our spirits stewed.

The flowers bloom in vibrant cheer,
Where merry hearts draw ever near,
In every petal, joy resides,
As hopes elate and love abides.

From babbling brooks to towering trees,
The world's alive with symphonies,
In every rustle, every sigh,
A promise made to never die.

So gather 'round, both young and old,
In merriment, let stories unfold,
As nature dances, wild and free,
In verdant whispers, we shall be.

The Dance of Fantastical Flora

In twilight's embrace, they sway and twirl,
Petals aglow with a magical whirl.
Their vibrant hues cast shadows bright,
A living ballet in the soft, moonlight.

Beneath the gaze of the ancient trees,
Whispers of secrets dance on the breeze.
In harmony, they weave through the air,
Enchanting all with a fragrant flare.

Delicate voices rise, soft and clear,
Inviting the wanderers to draw near.
Each blossom a story, each leaf a song,
In the heart of the woods, where dreams belong.

With every flutter, magic unfolds,
In the petals that shimmer like threads of gold.
The dance of the flora, a wondrous sight,
Capturing hearts in the tranquil night.

So lose yourself in this vibrant trance,
Where every moment is a fleeting chance.
Join the dance 'neath the heavenly glow,
Where the fantastical flora freely flow.

Beneath the Glistening Canopy

In a hidden world where the shadows weave,
The shimmering leaves gently breathe.
Light filters down through branches above,
As nature sings a hymn of love.

Mystic creatures roam and glide,
With secrets and stories they cannot hide.
In every nook, enchantment thrives,
Beneath the canopy, wonder survives.

The air is thick with scents divine,
Of blooming flowers on ancient vine.
Soft murmurs echo, a soft serenade,
An orchestra played in the glade.

Time drifts slowly, wrapped in delight,
Beneath the glistening stars of night.
A lullaby sung by the wise old trees,
Brings solace and peace with the gentlest breeze.

So linger awhile in this magical space,
Let the beauty of nature embrace.
For in the shadows and light's gentle sway,
The heart of the forest calls us to stay.

Woven in Starlit Threads

In midnight's glow, the world seems to pause,
A tapestry woven with nature's laws.
Stars above twinkle, bright and clear,
Weaving dreams for the wanderers near.

Each whispering leaf holds a tale of old,
Secrets of magic yet to be told.
In the darkened woods, starlight weaves,
A path of enchantment for those who believe.

Crickets sing as the moon takes flight,
Guiding lost souls through the velvety night.
Every shadow a guardian, strong and true,
In the realm where the extraordinary grew.

With each heartbeat, the forest hums,
A chorus of life as twilight comes.
Boundless wonder in the air we share,
Woven in starlit threads, a celestial affair.

So wander, dear dreamers, beneath the sky,
Where the threads of the cosmos knot and tie.
Embrace the magic, let your spirit soar,
In the arms of the night, forever explore.

The Heartbeat of the Wonder Woods

In the heart of the woods, a soft heartbeat thrums,
Where whispers of magic flow like soft plums.
Trees stand tall, guardians wise,
Keeping the secrets beneath the skies.

With every rustle, stories awaken,
Of creatures and fairies, history unshaken.
Sunlight dances on leaves of green,
A glimpse of the wonders yet to be seen.

Emerald shades wrapped in twilight's glow,
Breath of the forest, soft winds that blow.
Echoes of laughter, a gentle refrain,
A harmony found in the sweet summer rain.

Amidst the ferns, dreams intertwine,
Threads of enchantment in every design.
In this realm where time skips and bends,
The heartbeat of wonder never ends.

So journey with joy through these sylvan plains,
Let the heartbeat of the woods ease your pains.
For here in the magic, so vibrant and deep,
Lies the heart of the wonder, a treasure to keep.

Legends of the Fabled Pastures

In pastures green where shadows play,
Old tales whisper, night and day.
The wind it carries secrets bold,
Of heroes brave and hearts of gold.

By streams that dance in silver light,
The tales of valor take to flight.
Each blade of grass holds stories deep,
Of sleepless nights and dreams we keep.

Beneath the boughs of elder trees,
The echoes hum upon the breeze.
Through realms of magic, fate unfolds,
The legends spun, forever told.

With starlit skies as witness true,
Adventures blossom—old, yet new.
In every rustle, every sound,
The heart of lore is tightly bound.

So wanderers, with hearts ablaze,
Seek fabled paths, in twilight's haze.
For in the fields where shadows cast,
You'll find the legends of the past.

Shadows of Celestial Beasts

In realms where starlight softly gleams,
Celestial beasts weave ancient dreams.
With wings of dusk and eyes like fire,
They navigate the realms of higher.

From heights unknown, they soar and glide,
In whispers low, their secrets hide.
A tapestry of night they weave,
In mystic forms, they dance and leave.

With patterns drawn across the skies,
They chart the course of fate's goodbyes.
Through lunar glow, their shadows creep,
In silence deep, their secrets keep.

With howls that echo through the night,
They guard the paths of dreamers' flight.
In tales of old, their spirits soar,
The shadows call, forevermore.

So tread with care where starlight bleeds,
For in the dark, the essence feeds.
In every rustle, soft and fleet,
The celestial heart gives time a beat.

Beneath the Canopy of Whimsy

Beneath the leaves of fabled trees,
Where laughter dances with the breeze,
The world is stitched with dreams and schemes,
Entwined in silken, golden beams.

A tapestry of color bright,
In shades that twinkle, pure delight.
The magic hums, a gentle song,
Inviting all to wander long.

With creatures strange and wonders rare,
They beckon forth with playful care.
In every nook and corner hid,
A spark of joy in life, well bid.

Through twirling paths of fairytale,
The echoes of enchantment sail.
As shadows stretch and daylight wanes,
Adventures flourish, free from chains.

So come, dear friend, and leave your load,
For underneath this wise abode,
You'll find in dreams and laughter spun,
The whimsical and wild, as one.

The Elusive Paths of Enchantment

Within the woods where shadows twine,
The paths of magic intertwine.
With every step, a secret blooms,
A fragrant dance that sweetly looms.

The moonlight guides the wayward lost,
Through whispered woods at any cost.
The air is thick with wonder's kiss,
A call to those who seek the bliss.

Each turn reveals a hidden gate,
To realms beyond, where hearts elate.
The stars above like lanterns bright,
Illuminate the paths of night.

With riddles spun by unseen hands,
In every corner, magic stands.
A flicker here, a glow over there,
The essence wraps you in its care.

So wander forth with open eyes,
And let your heart embrace the skies.
For in the dance of fate and chance,
The paths of enchantment bid you glance.

Blooming Legends in Twilight

In twilight's glow, the petals sway,
Whispered tales in skies of gray.
Each flower speaks of ancient lore,
Secrets kept from days of yore.

The fading light, a gentle kiss,
A moment caught in fleeting bliss.
Legends bloom where shadows creep,
In heart's embrace, their stories seep.

Dewdrops hold the stars' soft light,
Magic glows in the fall of night.
A waltz of colors, bold and bright,
Guiding dreams to take their flight.

Beneath the branches, time stands still,
The air is thick with fragrant thrill.
Each leaf a promise, every stem,
A map to realms beyond our ken.

In twilight's hush, the earth bestows,
A dance of life where wonder grows.
With every breath, we find the rhyme,
In blooming legends, lost in time.

A Harmony of Enchanted Flora

Where lilies sway in softest breeze,
In hidden nooks, they find their ease.
An orchestra of colors bright,
Sings of magic in the light.

Through lush green paths, the fairies flit,
As petals dance in perfect wit.
Their laughter echoes through the glade,
A harmony the night has made.

Old roots entwine in whispered song,
Inviting all who pass along.
The fragrant blooms, a sweet perfume,
Awakening the night's soft gloom.

In every bud, a tale unfolds,
Of brave adventures, heroes bold.
In fragrant dreams, our hopes take flight,
With nature's magic, pure delight.

A tapestry of life we weave,
In every leaf, our hearts believe.
A harmony of enchanted glow,
In flora's grace, our spirits grow.

Secrets of the Hidden Glade

In shadows deep, where silence weaves,
The hidden glade conceals its leaves.
With secrets wrapped in emerald hue,
A world of wonders, known to few.

The ancient trees in wisdom stand,
Guardians of this sacred land.
Their roots entwined, a tale unfolds,
Of magic lost and legends told.

Moonlight spills on petals wide,
As whispers ride the evening tide.
In hushed tones, the nightingale sings,
Carrying dreams on silver wings.

Among the ferns, where fairies play,
In veils of mist, they softly sway.
Their laughter mingles with the breeze,
Secrets hidden among the trees.

A chance encounter, if you're bold,
Might uncover treasures untold.
The glade awaits with open arms,
For those who seek its quiet charms.

The Allure of Mythical Pastures

Beyond the hills where shadows chase,
Lie pastures dressed in nature's grace.
With whispers soft, the breezes call,
To realms where ancient spirits thrall.

In golden fields where starlight spills,
The air is sweet with blooming thrills.
Mythical chants ride on the air,
Enchanting hearts of those who dare.

A grazing herd of fae and kin,
With eyes that spark, their tales begin.
A tapestry of time entwined,
With every hoofprint, fate aligned.

The horizon painted, dusk to dawn,
In vibrant hues, new dreams are drawn.
With every step, the past ignites,
In mythical pastures, pure delights.

So wander forth, with open mind,
Seek visions of the rarest kind.
In every blade of grass, you'll find,
The allure of tales that bind.

Starlit Verses from the Enchanted Vale

In the vale where shadows dance,
Stars twinkle in a secret trance.
Whispers of the night unfold,
Tales of magic softly told.

Misty paths of silver glow,
Guided by the moon's soft flow.
Gentle breezes weave their song,
In this world where dreams belong.

Crickets chirp a lullaby,
As the night begins to sigh.
Fireflies blink in fleeting flight,
Painting stories in the night.

Hidden glades with ancient trees,
Swaying softly in the breeze.
Each leaf hums a timeless rhyme,
Binding hearts with threads of time.

Beneath the canopy of stars,
Adventure waits, no door ajars.
Every heartbeat sings of grace,
In this starlit, sacred space.

Whimsy Beneath the Emerald Sky

Beneath the sky of vibrant green,
Lies a world of wonder seen.
Laughter bubbles, tickles air,
In a land of giggles rare.

Fluffy clouds like cotton candy,
Drift above the hills so dandy.
Flowers dance in colors bright,
Painting smiles in pure delight.

Squirrels chat in playful jest,
As the sun sets in the west.
With each breeze, the treetops sway,
Whimsy reigns in bright array.

Secrets find their way to light,
In the soft and dusky night.
Every shadow, every gleam,
Whispers softly of a dream.

With each dawn, new joys arise,
Underneath the emerald skies.
In this realm where heartbeats play,
Whimsy holds the night at bay.

Faerie Dreams in the Dew-kissed Grass

In the glen where faeries dwell,
Dew-kissed grass weaves magic's spell.
Twinkling lights in shades so rare,
Sprinkle dreams upon the air.

Mushrooms dance in vibrant hues,
Where the morning softly brews.
Every petal, every breeze,
Tells a tale that never flees.

Gnarly roots and hidden nooks,
Glimmer gently like old books.
Whispers echo, soft and low,
In the places few will go.

Nightingales sing sweet and clear,
Drawing hearts that wander near.
In this world of glimmering light,
Faerie dreams take gentle flight.

Every step a dance of grace,
Through the magic's warm embrace.
Here beneath the dewdrops' glass,
We find peace in nature's pass.

Fantasies Woven in Nature's Quilt

In the woods where tales are spun,
Nature's quilt shines in the sun.
Leaves like pages, stories told,
In the warmth of threads of gold.

Rivers murmur songs of lore,
Whispers heard from ancient shore.
Every creature plays its part,
Weaving wonders, heart to heart.

Mountains stand with heads held high,
Underneath a painted sky.
Dreamers roam with hearts set free,
In the realms of fantasy.

Mornings bring a golden fire,
Filling souls with bright desire.
Each moment crafted, pure delight,
In the tapestry of light.

As the day draws to a close,
Stars emerge like blooming rose.
In this quilt of night and day,
Fantasies forever play.

The Lullaby of Wildflower Serenades

In meadows wide where wildflowers sway,
The whispers of breezes sing soft and gay.
Petals dance with the light of the morn,
Each note a promise, a new day reborn.

Beneath the canopy, shadows play,
Butterflies flutter, a soft ballet.
Gentle streams weave their silver thread,
To lull the earth, where dreams are bred.

As sun dips low, skies brim with gold,
Nature spins tales that never grow old.
Crickets chirp in the twilight's embrace,
A lullaby sweet, a warm, tender space.

With starlit twinkles, the night takes flight,
The hush of the world cradles the night.
In the quiet, soft secrets are spun,
As wildflowers sleep, their day comes undone.

So listen close, to the serenade sung,
Each note a treasure, where heartstrings are strung.
In the dance of the wild, let your spirit roam,
For here in this haven, you're never alone.

Radiant Mysteries in the Glimmering Grove

In a grove where whispers weave through the trees,
Golden light flickers in the gentle breeze.
Secrets are nested in shadows so deep,
Where nightingales sing as the world drifts to sleep.

Ferns embrace stories long left untold,
While moonlight sprawls, draping silver and gold.
The tapestry glimmers, each thread a delight,
Mysteries dance in the hush of the night.

Awake in the stillness, the stars hold the key,
Unlocking the magic of all that can be.
Amidst the silence, hearts start to soar,
In the glimmering grove, find what's in store.

A flicker, a shimmer, the night's gentle sigh,
Echoes of dreams in the wide, velvety sky.
Enchanting the senses, the night brings a grace,
Unraveling riddles in time and in space.

So linger a while in this sacred retreat,
Breathe in the wonders, let your heart beat.
For in this grove where the mysteries reign,
A radiant journey begins once again.

Intrigues of the Pastoral Dawn

As dawn unfurls her soft, silken shawl,
The whispers of morning beckon us all.
With each tender ray, a story will bloom,
Over fields that awaken from night's gentle gloom.

The lark takes to skies, its song taking flight,
Haunting the echoes of fading twilight.
Every dewdrop beams with the sun's warm caress,
Each blade of grass dons its diamond-dress.

Hillsides rise gently, bathed in the light,
Where shadows devour the remnants of night.
In the distance, the barn owls retreat,
While the sun declares victory, steadfast and sweet.

Crisp echoes of laughter ripple the streams,
Filling the air with the sweetness of dreams.
As nature awakens, so too does our heart,
In the pastoral dawn, we each play a part.

Let time be a canvas, painted in gold,
The intrigues unfold as the day starts to mold.
In the glow of the morning, we find what is true,
A tapestry woven in fresher hues.

The Allure of Celestial Territory

In the hush of the cosmos, dreams softly twine,
Constellations whisper, their secrets divine.
Galaxies swirl in a timeless embrace,
Each star an invitation, a luminous trace.

Nebulae drape in their colors so rare,
A dance of the heavens, beyond all compare.
Cosmic threads weave tales in the night,
Of wonders unseen, of endless flight.

On the edge of the universe, thoughts take their wing,
In the canvas of silence, the heart starts to sing.
Gravity bows to the lightness of dreams,
Where the allure of the stars gently gleams.

With each shooting star, wishes take flight,
Devotion to wonders that twinkle at night.
In the silence of space, we find our own worth,
Connected forever to the magic of Earth.

So gaze at the heavens, let your spirit play,
In this celestial territory, let souls sway.
For in each tiny spark that shimmers so bright,
Lives the allure of the boundless night.

A Tapestry of Ethereal Sights

In twilight's hue the shadows play,
A tapestry of dreams in gray.
Stars whisper secrets, soft and bright,
Weaving wonders into the night.

A silken thread, the moon does spin,
Glimmers of joy where hope begins.
Among the branches, shadows dart,
Each fleeting moment, a work of art.

The breeze carries tales, so divine,
Of ancient paths where fates entwine.
In gentle sighs, the echoes ring,
The magic of dawn in every spring.

In every flicker, the world awakes,
New realms of wonder each heartbeat makes.
A tapestry crafted with love and care,
The heart beats louder in the midnight air.

So venture forth, into the gleam,
Where life and dreams entwine and teem.
A dance of light, of shadowed might,
In the tapestry spun from the depths of night.

The Dance of Light on Meadow's Edge

Upon the lush where wildflowers sway,
The sun breaks forth to greet the day.
A gentle waltz in golden beams,
Awakening the meadow's dreams.

Beneath the oak, a world set free,
With whispers soft as a honeyed bee.
The light pirouettes, enchanting grace,
In nature's arms, a warm embrace.

The dewdrops glisten, a jeweled crown,
As petals flutter, twirling down.
In every glimpse, a story spun,
The dance of light has just begun.

Beneath the arches of sky so vast,
Every moment present, every shadow past.
In verdant fields where spirits roam,
The light recalls us, guiding home.

So linger here, let worries cease,
In nature's dance, we find our peace.
With every heartbeat, every breath,
In this meadowed realm, embrace the zest.

Shimmering Dreams among the Grasses

In twilight's hush, a shimmer glows,
Among the grasses, secret flows.
Where shadows bloom in silken thread,
And dreams arise from what is said.

The fireflies weave their glowing trails,
Each flicker speaks of ancient tales.
In whispers soft, the night bestows,
The tender heart where magic grows.

With starlit wishes, the breezes sing,
Echoes of joy that the night can bring.
Among the reeds, our laughter lies,
In shimmering dreams beneath the skies.

The moon reflects on silken streams,
As time unravels through our dreams.
A canvas painted with love's embrace,
In every heartbeat, we find our place.

So close your eyes and drift away,
For here in night, the shadows play.
In shimmering dreams, forever stay,
Among the grasses where spirits sway.

Timeless Mysteries of the Grove

In ancient woods where whispers dwell,
The timeless grove weaves its spell.
With every leaf and twisted vine,
A secret world, serene and divine.

The sunlight dances through the trees,
In harmony with the gentle breeze.
Each shadow holds a story untold,
Of magic deep and wonders bold.

The roots entwine in sacred ground,
Where echoes of the past resound.
In every bough, a life once lived,
Timeless mysteries the forest gives.

The creatures scurry in playful jest,
In nature's cradle, they find their rest.
With every footfall, a riddle unfolds,
In ancient realms where life beholds.

So wander softly, listen close,
For the grove will share what matters most.
In timeless whispers, the wisdom flows,
Among the trees, the magic grows.

Traces of Enchantment in Every Step

In whispers of the twilight breeze,
Where shadows dance 'neath ancient trees,
Each footprint holds a tale untold,
Of magic spun in threads of gold.

The gravel sings a secret tune,
As rays of light begin to swoon,
With every step, a spark ignites,
Awakening forgotten nights.

The echoes of a laughter sweet,
Resound in gardens where dreams meet,
While petals blush with dew-soaked gleam,
And magic lingers in the stream.

Through moonlit paths where spirits tread,
The stories of the stars are spread,
A tapestry of time so vast,
In every step, the die is cast.

So dance with shadows, light your way,
For every night fades into day,
And in the heart, pure wonder keeps,
As traces of enchantment sleeps.

Glittering Horizons of Myth

Beyond the veil where legends bloom,
A world awaits, dispelling gloom,
With forests deep and mountains high,
Beneath the ever-watchful sky.

The rivers glisten, winding free,
Reflecting tales of mystery,
Where creatures whisper in the night,
And shadows dance in silver light.

In ancient ruins, echoes call,
A hint of magic in the hall,
The dreams of those who've come before,
Gilded in myth forevermore.

With every dawn, a chance to see,
The glittering shores of fantasy,
A spark ignites in hearts anew,
Creating worlds in skies so blue.

So take a step into the haze,
Embrace the magic of these days,
For in adventures, stories swell,
And every myth has truth to tell.

Morning Dew and Magic's Kiss

Awake with dawn, the world still glows,
In morning's light, new magic flows,
The dew drops cling to blades of grass,
As time breathes soft, the moments pass.

Each petal holds a whispered prayer,
A promise made upon the air,
With every spark where sunlight plays,
A magic kiss begins the day.

The birds compose a gentle song,
Inviting hearts to sing along,
And in the whispers of the trees,
The magic dances on the breeze.

As shadows lengthen with the sun,
And dreams awaken, one by one,
The world's embrace, so warm and bright,
Paves paths of hope in morning light.

So greet the dawn with open arms,
For magic glows with all its charms,
In every breath, discover bliss,
In morning dew and magic's kiss.

Enchanted Paths of Lingering Dreams

Beneath a sky of twinkling stars,
We wander forth, forgetting scars,
In realms where dreams and wonders weave,
The heart believes what it can achieve.

The whispering winds of twilight call,
As shadows stretch and dip and fall,
Upon the paths of softest light,
Where magic blooms in every sight.

Each step we take, a tale unfolds,
In ancient forests, lost yet bold,
With every turn, the world awakes,
As lingering dreams find safer makes.

Through meadows bright and valleys deep,
Where secrets of the night we keep,
The stars align in patterns rare,
Guiding us onward, ever fair.

So let us roam where magic sings,
Embracing all that dreaming brings,
For life's a journey, wild and true,
On enchanted paths meant for me and you.

A Tapestry of Fabled Blossoms

In gardens where the whispers play,
The petals dance in bright array.
Each hue a tale from days of yore,
Of brave adventurers who sought for more.

Beneath the boughs of ancient trees,
Where secrets hum with gentle breeze,
The flowers twine their fragrant lore,
With stories woven evermore.

When twilight falls and shadows creep,
The blossoms guard the dreams we keep.
In twilight's glow, their magic glints,
And dreams unfurl like silken tints.

With every bloom, a spell is cast,
Of love, of joy, of forgotten past.
A tapestry of colors bright,
That hold the magic of the night.

So come, dear friend, and take your seat,
With petals soft and stories sweet.
For in this realm of fabled charm,
The heart finds peace, the soul finds balm.

Glimmers of the Enchanted Grove

In glades where gentle fairies glide,
The sunlight dappled, hearts collide.
With laughter light, the spirits play,
As twilight weaves the end of day.

The silver leaves catch whispers low,
Of wishes made where moonbeams flow.
Each flicker tells a tale an old,
Of magic dreams and treasures bold.

A path that winds through emerald hues,
Where every step a charm imbues.
Each glimmer sparkles, lighting guides,
To realms where ancient power bides.

The creatures stir, with eyes aflame,
In shadows where the secrets claim.
With every glance, the grove will sing,
A symphony of woodland spring.

So wander deep, let heart be free,
In this enchanted tapestry.
Where glimmers spark an ageless fire,
And every heart can find its choir.

Whimsy on Emerald Ground

Upon a field of emerald green,
Where dreams and laughter are often seen.
The daisies nod in playful dance,
Inviting hearts to join the trance.

With every breeze, a story spins,
Of splendor found in simple things.
The butterflies weave tales so bright,
In colors splashed by morning light.

A joy that twinkles in the air,
With sparkles full of light and care.
The whispers of the grass delight,
As children play till falls the night.

The clouds parade on azure skies,
As secrets gleam in children's eyes.
With every giggle, every sound,
A tapestry on emerald ground.

So join the dance, let worries fade,
In whimsy's arms, your heart displayed.
For in this valley, pure and true,
The magic lives in me and you.

A Frolic Beneath Celestial Canopies

Beneath the arch of starlit skies,
Where moonlight glows and magic lies.
The whispers of the night unfold,
As secrets in the dark are told.

With every twinkle, stories rise,
From dreams that drift in starry sighs.
A frolic where the wild things roam,
And every heart can find a home.

The silver shadows softly sway,
In rhythmic dance, they weave and play.
With laughter laced in twilight's breath,
A celebration of life and death.

The constellations blink and gleam,
Like echoes of a distant dream.
With every heartbeat, nature sings,
Of ancient tales and wondrous things.

So let us wander, hand in hand,
In this enchanted, endless land.
For beneath the celestial glow,
A frolic beckons, soft and slow.

Petals in the Mystical Grove

In twilight's cloak, the petals sway,
A dance of colors, bright and gay.
Whispers of magic fill the air,
As secrets linger everywhere.

The ancient trees, with wisdom vast,
Guard tales of love, both present and past.
Sunlight filters through leaves above,
A sacred place, a realm of love.

Each flower blooms a story told,
Of dreams they harbor, shy and bold.
Among the roots, the fairies play,
In shadows where the spirits stay.

The brook's soft song, a gentle guide,
In harmony with nature, they abide.
The petals whisper, soft and clear,
Of all that's sacred, drawing near.

So wander through this grove so bright,
And let your heart embrace the light.
For in each petal, magic flows,
In every shadow, wonder grows.

Echoes from the Faerie Domain

Amidst the glades, where shadows fall,
The faerie realm stands proud and tall.
With laughter ringing, soft and sweet,
Where time and dreamlike moments meet.

From moonlit glades, the echoes call,
In melodies that gently enthrall.
Beneath the stars, their secrets spill,
A dance of light, a silent thrill.

With wings that shimmer, faeries rise,
Casting spells beneath the skies.
Their glowing eyes, like polished stones,
Guard ancient tales, in hushed tones.

In every flutter, stories weave,
Of hopes, and dreams we all believe.
The gentle breeze, with whispers fraught,
Hints of the magic that can't be caught.

So make a wish upon a star,
For faeries listen, near and far.
With every breath, in twilight's gleam,
You'll find the echoes of your dream.

Beneath the Fabled Green

Where sunlight dapples, shadows play,
Beneath the fabled green array.
The forest hums a soothing tune,
Where mysteries dance beneath the moon.

The mossy paths, a hidden lore,
Invite the wanderer to explore.
Each step reveals, with every breath,
The whispers of life and gentle death.

In thicket dense, where wild things roam,
Nature cradles every home.
With rustling leaves, the secrets blend,
In harmony, where stories mend.

The petals fall, like dreams gone by,
In reverence, we stand and sigh.
For here beneath the fabled green,
A magic deep, forever seen.

So tread with care, embrace the peace,
Let your heart roam, and doubts release.
In every shade, in every hue,
Beneath the green, find love anew.

Secrets of the Hidden Pasture

In the hidden pasture, silence reigns,
Where ancient lore flows through the veins.
With every breeze, a story told,
Of secrets kept, and hearts of gold.

The wildflowers sway, a vibrant sea,
Holding whispers of what used to be.
In every blade, a memory weaves,
A tapestry that never leaves.

Among the stones, by the old oak tree,
Stories linger, wild and free.
The echoes of laughter, of youth's embrace,
Bring warmth and light to this sacred place.

With every sunset, colors blend,
Painting the sky as day must end.
In twilight's hush, the dreams ignite,
In the pasture's glow, all feels right.

So find your way to this meadow fair,
Where the past and present linger there.
For in its heart, the secrets lay,
Of lives entwined in nature's sway.

Whispers of Enchanted Meadows

In meadows green where fairies play,
A gentle breeze carries dreams away.
Soft petals dance in twilight's grace,
Nature's secrets find their place.

Moonlit paths through whispered trees,
Carry tales upon the breeze.
Each rustle sings of magic's bloom,
Inviting hearts to leave their gloom.

A brook glistens, laughter sweet,
Guiding lost souls on their feet.
Here, the stars seem close, they glow,
A world where dreams and wishes flow.

Shimmering flowers, colors bright,
Bathe in the glow of soothing light.
As shadows dance in gentle sway,
The meadows murmur, night and day.

Step softly now on emerald grass,
Where time itself seems slow to pass.
In enchanted meadows, hearts unite,
In the magic born of love's delight.

Shadows Beneath the Celestial Canopy

Underneath a sky so wide,
Stars ignite in cosmic tide.
Moonbeams weave through branches bare,
Casting shadows, filling air.

Whispers echo in the night,
Secrets held in silver light.
Starlit paths beckon the brave,
For dreams reside where shadows wave.

Clouds drift softly, a phantom chase,
Embracing mystery's warm embrace.
Crickets sing their nightly tune,
To twinkling stars and silver moon.

Glimmers dance on leaves so bright,
Leading wanderers with delight.
Beneath this canopy so grand,
Magic stirs, eternally planned.

In the silence, thoughts converge,
As the mind begins to surge.
Beneath the stars, we weave our fate,
In shadows deep, we navigate.

Secrets of the Glittering Glade

In the heart of woods so deep,
Glittering glades where fairies weep.
A hidden world where wonders sigh,
Where ancient trees reach for the sky.

Dewdrops nestle on mossy stone,
Each a promise, softly grown.
Rustling leaves tell tales untold,
Of magic lost and dreams of old.

Sunlight dapples through the green,
A sparkling dance on nature's sheen.
Elves with laughter weave their song,
In this haven where we belong.

Petals whisper secrets sweet,
Where paths converge and spirits meet.
In the glade, all woes dissolve,
As nature's heart begins to revolve.

So linger here where shadows play,
And let your doubts just fade away.
For in the glade, true magic lies,
In every breath, under wide skies.

The Unicorn's Veil of Dreams

In twilight's glow, a horned silhouette,
Dances softly, a figure we won't forget.
With every step, the world stands still,
As magic wraps us, a wondrous thrill.

Through silver mist, the unicorn glides,
A creature where purest magic abides.
With eyes of stars and coat of light,
It whispers dreams into the night.

In fields of gold, where visions grow,
Its presence lingers, a gentle flow.
A soft neigh calls to wandering hearts,
Guiding them where the journey starts.

Beneath the moon's enchanting gaze,
The unicorn leads through ethereal haze.
Each breath a wish, each hoof a beat,
In this realm, where wonder and beauty meet.

So close your eyes and take a chance,
For dreams await in a magical dance.
With the unicorn's veil, our spirits soar,
To a world of dreams forevermore.

Laughter Among Enchanted Greens

In the heart of the emerald glade,
Where echoes of joy softly wade,
Whispers of magic weave through the air,
As children of wonder lose all their care.

Sunlight dances on leaves like a dream,
With giggles and whispers, they form a stream,
Pixies flutter, their laughter so light,
Creating a symphony, pure and bright.

Under the canopy, secrets unfold,
Stories of heroes and legends once told,
Mushrooms like thrones for the fairies to rest,
In the heart of the forest, enchanted and blessed.

Breezes carry the scent of sweet blooms,
Curling around shadows that softly loom,
With each little giggle, a spell takes its form,
In the laughter of greens, all hearts feel warm.

As dusk paints the skies in hues of gold,
The laughter fades softly, leaves stories untold,
Yet deep in the woods, the magic remains,
In the laughter among enchanted greens, it reigns.

The Serenade of Wild Blossoms

In a meadow where wild blossoms sway,
A chorus of colors greets the day,
Petals like notes in a melody spun,
Beneath the warm kiss of the rising sun.

Daisies and poppies, a beautiful sight,
Swaying and shimmering, a pure delight,
With butterflies dancing, their wings all aglow,
In the serenade of wild blossoms, they flow.

Gentle breezes hum tunes of the earth,
Whispering tales of creation and birth,
Every bloom sings its unique refrain,
In gardens of magic where dreams break the chain.

Larks weave high on the soft azure sky,
Nature's own orchestra, soaring up high,
The petals keep time with the songs of the air,
As the wild blossoms sway, free of all care.

And when twilight wraps all in its grace,
The blossoms retreat, yet leave a warm trace,
For in the heart of the night, they will gleam,
And whisper their secrets, as if in a dream.

A Journey Through the Mythic Meadow

Through the mythic meadow where stories reside,
Adventures await with each stride,
Beneath ancient trees where wisdom is found,
An enchantment whispers, alive all around.

Crystal streams sparkle and giggle with glee,
Carving through roots of the grand willow tree,
Every twist and turn tells a tale of old,
As the dreams of the past in the present unfold.

Sunbeams weave blankets in patterns divine,
Where echoes of laughter and magic entwine,
Each flower a messenger, fragrant and bright,
In hues of the rainbow, a picturesque sight.

Frogs croak in rhythm, a symphony sweet,
While fireflies dance, weaving tales at their feet,
Beneath a sky painted with stars so grand,
Illuminating paths through this mystical land.

As shadows stretch long and the night does unfold,
The meadow keeps secrets too precious to hold,
For every journey invites one to see,
The magic that thrives in life's mystery.

Fables in Blooming Spectrum

In gardens of wonder, fables take flight,
With petals of stories painted in light,
Every bloom a whisper, a tale to explore,
In the heart of spring, nature's ancient lore.

Violets tell stories of dreams softly spun,
While roses reveal love beneath the bright sun,
Daffodils dance with a jubilant cheer,
As tales echo softly for all who draw near.

With bees as the scribes, they pen all the rhymes,
In a language of nectar, transcending all times,
Where blossoms remember the stories they share,
Enchanting each heart with kindness and care.

As moonlight whispers on petals so fair,
The fables awaken and linger in air,
In hues of the twilight, the spectrum will gleam,
Marking the borders of night and of dream.

So wander the gardens where fables abide,
Let each blooming treasure be your faithful guide,
In the blooming spectrum of life's grand design,
Find tales that unite, and hearts that align.